# SECRETS & CELEBRATIONS
# LONDON

**Publisher and Creative Director:** Nick Wells
**Project Editor and Picture Research:** Sara Robson
**Art Director:** Mike Spender
**Layout Design:** Dave Jones
**Digital Design and Production:** Chris Herbert

**Special thanks to:** Eileen Cox, Helen Crust, Alexandra Davidson, Anna Groves, Digby Smith and Catherine Taylor

This edition first published 2012 by
**FLAME TREE PUBLISHING**
Crabtree Hall, Crabtree Lane
Fulham, London SW6 6TY
United Kingdom

www.flametreepublishing.com

12 14 16 15 13

1 3 5 7 9 10 8 6 4 2

Flame Tree is part of Flame Tree Publishing Limited

© 2012 Flame Tree Publishing Limited

A CIP record for this book is available from the British Library.

ISBN: 978-0-85775-374-8

Every effort has been made to contact copyright holders. We apologize in advance for any omissions and
would be pleased to insert the appropriate acknowledgement in subsequent editions of this publication.

Printed in China

### ACKNOWLEDGEMENTS

**Michael Robinson** (author) is an art historian by profession but is also a qualified London Blue Badge tour guide.
Born and raised in London, he cannot remember a time when his own natural curiosity was not evident, exploring the history and culture
of the city, leading inevitably to a passion for it that he still retains today, half a century later. Michael regards guiding as a vocation,
and enjoys sharing his passion for the city with tourists from all over the world. You can visit him at www.michaelgrobinson.com.

**Andy Williams** (photographer) studied photography at Guildford School of Art. He is acknowledged to be one of Britain's foremost
landscape photographers, and pictures from his library have appeared in books, brochures, calendars, greetings cards and posters all over the world.
He uses a 5 x 4 inch camera with lenses from 65 mm to 500 mm for his landscape and architecture photography, but also has a 6 x 7 cm outfit
for, as he puts it, 'anything that moves'. He is totally dedicated to his profession and strives to produce beautiful images of the world about us,
concentrating his skills mainly in the United Kingdom, where nothing gives him greater pleasure than to record on film the ever-changing moods
of nature. So if you come across a small man waiting patiently beside a large camera atop a tripod, you will know it is 'the happiest man he knows'!

Images courtesy of **Andy Williams**: 1, 4(c), 4(r), 7, 15, 16, 17, 18–19, 20, 21, 22–23, 24, 25, 26, 27, 28, 29, 30, 31, 32–33, 34, 35, 36–37, 38, 39, 41, 42, 43,
44, 45, 46, 47, 48–49, 50, 54–55, 56, 57, 58, 59, 60–61, 62, 63, 64, 65, 66–67, 68, 69, 70–71, 72, 78, 79, 80, 81, 82, 83, 84, 85, 86–87, 89, 90, 91, 92–93, 94,
97, 110, 111, 115, 117, 118, 119, 123, 124, 125, 139, 142, 143, 147, 153, 156, 157, 160, 161, 162, 164, 166–67, 168, 169, 173, 175, 178, 179, 181, 184, 185,
186, 187, 188–89. Courtesy of **Alamy** (www.alamy.com) and the following photographers: Greg Balfour Evans: 9, 176–77; Mike Hughes: 96; JLImages: 152; Thomas
Dryden Kelsey: 180; Grant Rooney: 165; Patricia Spinelli: 120–21. Courtesy of **Shutterstock** (www.shutterstock.com) and the following photographers: Piiotr
Adamski: 100; AISPIX: 5(r), 134, 158–59, 174; allylondon: 105; Dan Breckwoldt: 88; Michelle Brown: 163; Maksim Budnikov: 3, 114; Stephen Bures: 5(c), 136;
Jo Chambers: 116; Deymos: 140–41; Elena Elisseeva: 146; ffolas: 77; Stephen Finn: 8, 128, 154–55; Nadia Gerbish: 138; godrick: 95, 182–83; Matt Gore: 108–09;
Chris Harvey: 40, 192; Ihervas: 112–13; Thomas Owen Jenkins: 51; jennyt: 170–71; Kamira: 5(l), 102–03, 144–45, 148; Irina Korshunova: 106; Neil Lang: 104;
Nando Machado: 137; mary416: 107; Iain McGillivray: 4(l), 74–75; Chris Mole: 101; Monkey Business Images: 73; Daniel Nachtigall: 149; nagib: 126–27;
r.nagy: 129; sajko: 14; Rui Saraiva: 76; Fedor Selivanov: 6, 135, 172; St Nick: 12–13; Anibal Trejo: 132–33; David Young: 122.

# SECRETS & CELEBRATIONS
# LONDON

Michael Robinson

**FLAME TREE
PUBLISHING**

# Contents

6

# Introduction

THE WRITER AND LEXICOGRAPHER SAMUEL JOHNSON (1709–84) IS REPUTED TO HAVE SAID, 'WHEN A MAN IS TIRED OF LONDON, HE IS TIRED OF LIFE'. ALTHOUGH STATED OVER 200 YEARS AGO, THE SENTIMENT IS STILL RELEVANT AS THE CITY CONTINUES TO EVOLVE AND RE-INVENT ITSELF. TODAY LONDON IS ARGUABLY THE MOST COSMOPOLITAN CITY IN THE WORLD, WITH ESTIMATES THAT IT IS POSSIBLE TO HEAR OVER 300 LANGUAGES SPOKEN ON ITS STREETS. ONE SHOULD NOT BE TOO SURPRISED AT THIS STATISTIC, AS IT HAS BEEN HOME TO ECONOMIC AND POLITICAL MIGRANTS FOR SEVERAL CENTURIES.

This is not a history book *per se*, but one cannot appreciate London's secrets and celebrations without at least providing a context. Its story begins with the invasion of Britain by the Romans in AD 43 and the creation of Londinium as its capital 20 years later. It was chosen for its location on the River Thames and its access out to sea, making it an ideal trading port to the rest of the Roman Empire. The lowest fording point was at London Bridge, where the Romans built the first crossing point, establishing the city on the northern bank. Within a hundred years they had built a fort to house a legion of one thousand troops to maintain law and order, a site that is coincidentally now occupied by the headquarters of the City of London Police.

While there are only a few standing remnants of Roman London, it is important to recognize their legacy. The Romans established a road network, which is still used today – for example, Oxford St was originally part of a Roman road with an east-west axis. Many buildings such as Apsley House have Roman stylistic precedents, as does Marble Arch, which is based on the Arch of Constantine in Rome. The ovoid shape of the Royal Albert Hall can trace its shape to the Roman amphitheatre that once stood in Londinium on the site of what is now Guildhall. London is also culturally indebted to the Romans, with William Shakespeare (1564–1616) penning many of his plays and poems based on the writings of Virgil (70 BC–19 BC) and Ovid (43 BC–AD 18), a prime example being *A Midsummer Night's Dream*, which was inspired by Ovid's *Metamorphoses*.

When the Romans left in the fifth century, various warring factions from Saxony and Scandinavia plundered Britain until the Norman Conquest of 1066, when William of Normandy (1028–1087) became King of England, arguably the most pivotal moment in London's history. William, determined to cement his hold on his new kingdom, established his court at Westminster, and began a process of castle building on an unprecedented scale, including the White Tower at the Tower of London, completed in 1080 as a defensive stronghold and as a means of watching over the Londoners whom he mistrusted. Over the next 200 years the Tower was enlarged, becoming the formidable castle we see today. Over the centuries it has been a fortress, the royal observatory, a royal palace, the mint and, notoriously, a prison and place of execution. Today it is a major tourist attraction, where the Crown Jewels can be viewed and where one can get a sense of the Tower's often brutal history. William and his successors were also responsible for reinforcing the old Roman wall that was built around the city.

London continued to prosper financially from trade and the export of wool in the medieval period despite the Black Death (1348–50), a plague that claimed about half of London's 80,000-strong population. The Dissolution of the Monasteries (1536–41) radically altered the infrastructure of certain institutions in the sixteenth century, but again London continued to prosper commercially, particularly in the reign of Elizabeth I (1533–1603), when the merchant classes came of age. During the English Civil War of the

1640s, King Charles I (1600–49) was banished from his palace at Whitehall and forced into exile at Oxford where he set up court. Charles' demise took place in London, where he was found guilty of high treason and beheaded in Whitehall.

The next significant chapter in London's history was the Great Fire of 1666, which began in a bakery in the old city and, fanned by high winds, spread rapidly among the old wooden buildings. The failure of the Lord Mayor to act early enough resulted in nearly two thirds of the old city being destroyed, including the old St Paul's Cathedral. Rebuilding the city began slowly due to discussions about the street layout. England's greatest architect, Sir Christopher Wren (1632–1723), was appointed the King's Surveyor in 1669 and, although his plans for the layout of the city were rejected, he was given the task of rebuilding most of the churches and creating his masterpiece St Paul's Cathedral in the new Baroque style that he made his own. By this time London was enjoying unprecedented wealth and vying with the French court in terms of its lavishness. By the middle of the nineteenth century it had overtaken Paris and had become the capital of the most powerful nation in the world commercially, economically and militarily. The Great Exhibition of 1851, the first of the World's Fairs, reflected this

confidence, its success facilitating the development of government educational institutions in the arts and sciences, including the South Kensington Museum (later the Victoria and Albert Museum, or V&A). The success was in large part due to the efforts of the civil servant Sir Henry Cole (1808–82), whose organizational skills were exemplary and who went on to create many of the august bodies that are part of his legacy, including the Royal College of Art and the Royal College of Music. One of the wings of the V&A building is named in his honour.

The British Empire, which included India, Canada and Australia, as well as large parts of Africa, also had an effect on some of London's structures and infrastructure. Until the nineteenth century, the London docks were confined to the

Pool of London around the Tower of London area. The huge volume of shipping caused chaos, with foodstuffs perishing due to the length of time taken to unload, and gave rise to increasing levels of cargo theft. The decision was made to create a new docks area that began in 1802, east of the city further down river where large basins could be cut to accommodate the large ships. This development continued well into the twentieth century as the docks expanded.

Between the autumn of 1940 and May 1941, the docks were severely damaged by the strategic bombing of the area by the German Luftwaffe in the Blitz. In one night alone over a quarter of a million tons of timber were destroyed in the Surrey Docks. Equally devastating was the continual bombing of other areas of the capital, particularly in the old city where nearly four fifths of the buildings were destroyed. In December 1940, the Luftwaffe used mainly incendiary bombs and created what became known as 'The Second Great Fire of London'. In other parts of London, the House of Commons was wrecked and many other key buildings were damaged, including Buckingham Palace and the British Museum. London was also severely hit during the latter years of the war, when the Germans began their V-1 and V-2 rocket offensives.

The rebuilding of London was a matter of high priority, particularly for housing and business premises. Unfortunately little attention was paid to aesthetics in the building of many commercial properties, the need to build quickly and cheaply resulting in the creation of bland and, at times, what came to be known as Brutalist buildings. One of the most notable of these developments was Paternoster Row next to St Paul's Cathedral. It became something of an embarrassment to the

authorities, and many of these buildings have been, and continue to be, demolished and replaced by new exciting urban developments such as the 'Gherkin', using new and innovative ways of sustainable and green building techniques.

Tourists expect a good visitor experience, complemented by high-quality services in hotels and restaurants. This has led to substantial improvements in the capital, most notably in its buildings and streets, which are arguably the cleanest of any city in the world. Londoners hold a genuine pride in their city and there is an air of optimism that continues to evolve. It is most noticeable as the city plans for the 2012 Olympic Games, not just for the event itself, but also for a legacy involving the most radical urban development of an inner-city location anywhere. Samuel Johnson would have approved.

# Historical London

THIS SECTION EXAMINES A NUMBER OF SITES IN AND AROUND LONDON THAT MAP THE EXTRAORDINARY PANOPLY OF HISTORICAL EVENTS IN ENGLAND, FROM ROMAN TIMES TO THE PRESENT DAY. THE EMPHASIS IS VERY MUCH ON THE CITIES OF LONDON AND WESTMINSTER, WHERE MOST OF THE EVENTS WERE STAGED, BUT EXTENDS TO THE SUBURBS OF RICHMOND IN THE SOUTH-WEST AND GREENWICH IN THE SOUTH-EAST, WHERE KINGS AND QUEENS OF ENGLAND HAD THEIR WEEKEND RETREATS.

The old City of London was the commercial centre, as is the present-day City of London, but in the medieval period it was also an area densely populated with monasteries and churches. The Romans, seen in the eleventh century as pagan barbarians, founded the old walled city, and so King Edward the Confessor (c. 1003–66) decided to found a monastery in an uninhabited area that he called Westminster, building the first abbey on the site, consecrated in 1065. Close by he also established the beginnings of the Palace of Westminster. This area was developed as the seat of power, with other palaces built for subsequent sovereigns, and government offices being established after the English Civil War, when power was gradually devolved from monarchy to Parliament.

# Hampton Court Palace
## RICHMOND

The picture shows the magnificent eastern façade of the palace, designed by England's greatest architect, Sir Christopher Wren, for King William III (1650–1702) and Mary II (1662–94). Wren had to knock down the old Tudor palace of King Henry VIII (1491–1547), but for various reasons the work was not completed in the new style and much of the old palace remains, including Henry's magnificent Great Hall, complete with original tapestries. It is also possible to visit the vast Tudor kitchens that provided meals for the 1,200-strong household. The palace is unique in its forging of two very distinct styles.

# Kew Palace

### RICHMOND

The origins of Kew Palace can be traced back to the Elizabethan era (1558–1603), when the old palace was given as a gift to Robert Dudley (1532–88), the queen's favourite courtier. The present palace was built in the seventeenth century by a wealthy Flemish merchant; it was then acquired by King George II (1683–1760), and continued to be a royal residence until his grandson, George III (1738–1820) last used it in 1816. He used the palace as a retreat away from the London scene during his frequent bouts of insanity.

# Royal Hospital Chelsea

### KENSINGTON AND CHELSEA

Completed in 1692, the building was intended as a hospital and retirement home for former army personnel (non-officers), who were either destitute or disabled. The English Civil Wars (1642–51) highlighted the need for this provision, and the first 476 'Chelsea Pensioners' moved in to their new accommodation. During the nineteenth century the building was enlarged, although there are now only about 300 Chelsea Pensioners on site. This number also includes women soldiers, admitted since 2009. Additionally there are a number of so-called 'Out-Pensioners', who can often be seen on the streets of London in their distinctive red uniforms.

# Chapel of the Royal Hospital Chelsea

## KENSINGTON AND CHELSEA

The magnificent chapel was also designed by Wren and includes the large half-dome mural of the Resurrection by Sebastiano Ricci (1659–1734), painted in 1714. As with most of Wren's work, no expense was spared on the internal decoration, which has splendid examples of plasterwork and woodcarving. Originally, Chelsea Pensioners attended twice-daily compulsory services in the chapel, but today it is now only on Sundays when they assemble on parade in front of the building. The first-ever church service to be televised was broadcast from the chapel in 1949.

# Kensington Palace

## KENSINGTON AND CHELSEA

King William III suffered from asthma and needed a palace close enough to London for his official engagements, but removed from the smoky atmosphere of the city. Designed around the existing Nottingham House by Wren, Kensington Palace was home to the king and Queen Mary II until their respective deaths in 1702 and 1694. The palace remained a royal favourite, and it was used as the official residence of Diana, Princess of Wales, until her untimely death in 1997, and also by the present queen's younger sister, Margaret, until she died in 2002.

# Apsley House

## CITY OF WESTMINSTER

Standing on the edge of the park at Hyde Park Corner is the neoclassical former home of Arthur Wellesley, First Duke of Wellington (1769–1852), the great military commander who defeated the Emperor Napoleon at the Battle of Waterloo in 1815. It was originally known as Number One London, as it was the first house one passed coming into the city from the country at the Knightsbridge tollgate. The house was given to the nation by the seventh duke and is today the home of the Wellington Museum.

# Buckingham Palace
## CITY OF WESTMINSTER

Originally built for the Duke of Buckingham in the early eighteenth century, the property was acquired by King George III as a private residence for his wife, Queen Charlotte (1744–1818). The architect John Nash (1752–1835) enlarged the house for her son, the future George IV (1762–1830), but it did not become an official royal residence until 1837 and the beginning of the reign of Queen Victoria (1819–1901), who also continued to enlarge it. The famous façade with the balcony was added at the beginning of the twentieth century.

# St James's Palace
## CITY OF WESTMINSTER

Despite Buckingham Palace being the official residence for Her Majesty the Queen (b. 1926), St James's Palace is still the most senior royal palace in London. Ambassadors based in London are appointed to the Court of St James's, since it is where the Marshal of the Diplomatic Corps is resident. The palace was originally built for Henry VIII on the site of a former lepers' hospital, and the building is one of the city's few surviving Tudor buildings. King Charles I spent his last night at the palace before his execution in 1649.

# Horse Guards Parade

## CITY OF WESTMINSTER

The picture shows the ceremony of Trooping the Colour to mark the Queen's official birthday in June each year, when she inspects soldiers of the Household Division, who come together on the Horse Guards Parade at the rear of Whitehall. The ceremony has taken place since 1748, and is on the site of the old tiltyard that was part of Henry VIII's Whitehall Palace, largely destroyed by fire in 1698. The old guard house, which was also destroyed, was replaced in the 1750s and forms the spectacular buildings on the south side.

# Royal Horse Guard
## CITY OF WESTMINSTER

The Horse Guards of the Queen's Household Division are divided into two regiments, the Blues and Royals and the Life Guards, depicted here in their scarlet uniforms. They make up the two cavalry units of the Household Division and are part of a wider group that includes the five regiments of foot guards, who are part of the British Army's infantry. The Household Cavalry is mainly ceremonial and used as the sovereign's escort on state occasions. They can be seen mounting the guard each day at Horse Guards Parade.

# Houses of Parliament
## CITY OF WESTMINSTER

The current Houses of Parliament occupy the site that was once the palace of Westminster, established in the reign of King Edward the Confessor in the eleventh century. During the reign of Henry VIII, the royal palace was abandoned in favour of the newly built Whitehall Palace (since destroyed), and given to Parliament as a meeting place. In 1834 a huge fire destroyed most of the old palace buildings except for Westminster Hall and the fourteenth-century Jewel Tower. The rest was rebuilt to include the famous Westminster clock tower, affectionately known as 'Big Ben'.

# Statue of King Richard I
## CITY OF WESTMINSTER

Outside of the rebuilt House of Lords stands the statue of King Richard I, 'The Lionheart' (1157–99). Symbolically his sword is raised, since he spent most of his ten-year reign in the Holy Lands fighting during the Third Crusade, and was revered by his enemies as a fearsome warrior. He died without an heir to the throne and was succeeded by his younger brother John, ultimately responsible for endorsing the Magna Carta. The sculpture was created in the nineteenth century at a time when he was seen as a warrior defending the Christian cause.

# Statue of Sir Winston Churchill
## CITY OF WESTMINSTER

The statue in Parliament Square is one of several leading statesmen such as Sir Robert Peel, Nelson Mandela, Abraham Lincoln and David Lloyd-George, who in various ways have contributed towards the progress and maintenance of democracy. Churchill's statue faces the House of Commons, where he made many of his finest speeches before the Second World War, when he warned of Nazi oppression, and as Britain's Prime Minister during the conflict when it faced its 'darkest hour'. On his death in 1965, Churchill lay in state in Westminster Hall, an honour normally reserved for the Royal Family.

CHURCHILL

# No. 10 Downing Street

## CITY OF WESTMINSTER

The front door of No. 10 has a brass plate informing visitors that it is the office of the 'First Lord of the Treasury', despite the fact that the 'treasurer' or Chancellor of the Exchequer, the nearest equivalent, lives at No. 11. Historically, Robert Walpole (1676–1745), generally regarded as Britain's first Prime Minister, effectively held both positions as Lord of the Treasury and Chancellor of the Exchequer. Prior to this they were separate appointments made by the sovereign. The subsequent influence that Walpole had led to the pejorative use of the term 'prime minister'.

# Whitehall

## CITY OF WESTMINSTER

The street named Whitehall was once the site of a palace of the same name. Built in the reign of Henry VIII, it became the principal royal palace in London until it was destroyed in a fire in 1698. Henry built his palace after acquiring York Place from Cardinal Wolsey (1473–1530) following his fall from grace in 1530. When it was completed in the following century, it was the largest royal palace in Europe. The old wine cellars are currently beneath the Ministry of Defence building.

# Banqueting House at Whitehall

## CITY OF WESTMINSTER

The only building to survive the fire of 1698 was Banqueting House, designed by Inigo Jones (1573–1652) earlier in the century. The design, the first of its kind to be completed in London, is based on the classical proportions of the architect Andrea Palladio (1508–80) whom Jones had studied while in Italy in the early 1600s. The building was completed in 1622 in the reign of James I (1566–1625), the first of the Stuart kings. His son, who became Charles I, was executed on a scaffold erected outside the building on a cold January day in 1649.

# Westminster School

## CITY OF WESTMINSTER

Regarded as one of the top independent schools in Britain in terms of its academic record, Westminster is also one of the oldest. It was founded in 1179 as part of Westminster Abbey, when the Benedictine order provided tuition. The school was re-founded as The Royal College of St Peter at Westminster in 1560 by Queen Elizabeth I following the dissolution of the monasteries by her father Henry VIII. Among the school's notable alumni are Sir Christopher Wren, John Locke (1632–1704) and the writer A.A. Milne (1882–1954).

# Royal Courts of Justice

## CITY OF WESTMINSTER

The original royal courts were at Westminster Hall until this building was completed in 1882. The premises house the Court of Appeal and the High Courts of Justice, which is sub-divided into three separate divisions. One is the Family Division, which oversees matrimonial disputes, child welfare and probate matters as part of its remit. The proceedings in these courts are presided over by a High Court Judge, a senior rank in the British judicial system, and supervised by the Lord Chief Justice. George Edmund Street (1824–81) designed the buildings in the prevailing neo-Gothic style.

# Old Curiosity Shop

## CITY OF WESTMINSTER

The shop, as depicted here, was created as a result of the publication of the novel *The Old Curiosity Shop* in 1841 by Charles Dickens (1812–70). The owner of the premises at the time decided that Dickens had based his novel on the curiosity shop in Portsmouth Lane, Holborn, and wanted to capitalize on the fame the novel had generated. The premises date from 1567 and are among the capital's few surviving from that period.

# Lambeth Palace

## LAMBETH

Lambeth Palace is the London home of the Archbishop of Canterbury, the spiritual head of the Church of England. The oldest surviving parts of the palace are the chapel and Lollard's Tower, which dates from 1440, but the most striking part is the Tudor gatehouse built in red brick in 1495. The library, which dates from the early seventeenth century, is one of the oldest public libraries in England. The architect Edward Blore (1787–1879), who would later complete the work of John Nash at Buckingham Palace, enlarged Lambeth Palace in the 1830s.

# Globe Theatre

## SOUTHWARK

It was the vision and tenacity of the American filmmaker Sam Wanamaker (1919–93) that facilitated the rebuilding of the Globe Theatre close to its original site in Southwark. The original theatre was destroyed by fire in 1613 as a result of a cannon being fired which set light to the thatched roof during a performance of Shakespeare's play *Henry VIII*. It was rebuilt the following year but closed on the orders of Oliver Cromwell (1599–1658) in 1642 due to its less than puritanical performances. The present reconstruction was opened in 1997.

# Replica of
# *The Golden Hind*
## SOUTHWARK

Another reconstruction along the South Bank of the Thames is a replica of *The Golden Hind*, a galleon made famous by Sir Francis Drake (1540–96) and his circumnavigation of the world between 1577 and 1580. It was on this ship that Queen Elizabeth I bestowed a knighthood on Drake. The replica, launched in 1973, also circumnavigated the world, following Drake's route in 1979–80, and has made several other long-distance journeys. It is now in dry dock and used as an educational resource for schools.

# George Inn
## SOUTHWARK

Both Charles Dickens and William Shakespeare are known to have visited this galleried coaching inn, the only original one of its kind left in London. Dickens mentions 'The George' in his novel *Little Dorrit*. Originally the building, which dates back to at least 1542, was much larger but the railway demolished parts of it for its own expansion in 1899. Today the premises are still run as a public house but are owned by the National Trust, a charity that looks after many of Britain's historic properties.

# Temple Church
## CITY OF LONDON

Built by the Knights Templar in the twelfth century, the church is famous for its round nave. Traditionally new knights entered this nave through the west door at dawn to be initiated into the order prior to being sent to the Holy Land, where they would act as soldier-monks to protect pilgrims. A little over 100 years after the consecration of the church, the Templars were disbanded under the orders of the Pope, the church becoming the property of the Knights Hospitaller until the Dissolution.

# Old Bailey
## CITY OF LONDON

The present Central Criminal Court, known as the Old Bailey, was built on the site of the notorious Newgate Prison, where until 1868 public hangings were staged. The prison, in different incarnations, had been on the site since the twelfth century, and was finally demolished in 1902 to make way for the new session courthouse. The present building, which was extended between 1968 and 1972, has a large dome on which stands the figure representing Lady Justice, holding a sword in her left hand and the scales of justice in her right.

# Cloth Fair

## City of London

Since 1133, and every year until 1855, the three-day Cloth Fair beginning on 24 August had been held within the precincts of St Bartholomew's Monastery in Smithfield, even after the Dissolution. The fair attracted cloth merchants from all over Europe, and the Guild of Merchant Taylors would inspect the fabrics for quality before they were sold. Between the mid-seventeenth century and 1855 the fair became more riotous year on year and was eventually closed. The present street is named after the area within the monastic grounds where the fair was held.

# Guildhall

## City of London

Parts of the present building date to 1411 but it is widely assumed that it replaced an earlier building on the site. Guildhall is the administrative headquarters of the City of London where the Court of Common Council meet, as well as the venue for the annual election of the new Lord Mayor. It has also been used for some of the most famous trials in history, including those of the nine-day queen, Lady Jane Grey (1537–54), and Thomas Cranmer (1489–1556), Archbishop of Canterbury in the reign of Queen Mary I (1516–58), who refused to recant his Protestant faith.

# The Monument
## CITY OF LONDON

Designed by Sir Christopher Wren and his able assistant Robert Hooke (1635–1703), the Monument to the Great Fire of London, which occurred in September 1666, was completed in 1677. It stands 202 feet tall, the distance from the monument to the site of Thomas Farynor's bakery in Pudding Lane, where the fire started. Wren and Hooke also conceived the monument as a scientific laboratory in which barometric pressure could be measured, but they also designed the central shaft for experiments in gravity and included a zenith telescope.

# Tower of London
## TOWER HAMLETS

The central White Tower, clearly visible in the picture, forms the core of the Tower of London and was completed in 1080 by King William I, following his conquest of England in 1066. Over the next 200 years it was significantly enlarged by building two concentric walls around it that occupy some 12 acres of land. In its 900-year history it has been a royal palace, the location of the mint, a prison, a garrison, the royal observatory and a menagerie. It is most famous as the home of the Crown Jewels and the Yeoman Warders who guard them.

# *Cutty Sark*

## GREENWICH

This enormous clipper ship was one of several made in the nineteenth century for the transportation of tea from China to England. There was a need to build faster ships, as there were large bonuses paid to ship owners and crew to be the first back with their cargo. *Cutty Sark* was the last of the great tea clippers to be launched in 1869, and one of only two preserved for posterity. In 1890 she was used for general cargoes, ending her days as a stationary training ship, before being dry-docked in Greenwich.

# Old Royal Naval College

## GREENWICH

These magnificent buildings, designed by Wren and built by him and his pupil Nicholas Hawksmoor (1661–1736) after 1692, were not completed until after Wren's death in 1723. They were intended as a naval equivalent to the Royal Hospital in Chelsea, serving that purpose as the Royal Hospital for Seamen at Greenwich until 1863, when it became the Royal Naval College. It continued in that role until 1998, when parts of it were leased to the University of Greenwich and Trinity College of Music.

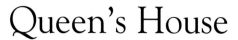

# Queen's House

## GREENWICH

The Queen's House at Greenwich was built in 1447 and was the birthplace of King Henry VIII and two of his children, Mary and Elizabeth. In the seventeenth century the palace was demolished, and the present house designed by Inigo Jones for Charles I as a summer retreat for his wife Henrietta Maria (1609–69). The work was not completed before the outbreak of the English Civil War, when Oliver Cromwell confiscated all royal properties. Work resumed after the Restoration, and was completed for Charles II's wife, Catherine of Braganza (1638–1705).

# Royal Observatory
## GREENWICH

The Royal Observatory was originally located at the Tower of London, and relocated to Greenwich in 1676, with the first Astronomer Royal Sir John Flamstead (1646–1719) living and working at the new location. Flamstead mapped over 3,000 celestial bodies, including the planet Uranus, which he mistook for a star. The building continued to be used as an observatory until the 1950s, when it relocated to Herstmonceux in Sussex due to increasing light pollution in London. Today it is a museum that charts the history of astronomy and the solution to the longitudinal problem.

# Eltham Palace
## GREENWICH

Originally Eltham was a royal palace used from the early fourteenth century, most notably by King Edward III (1312–77), until its demise during the Tudor period when it was only used as a hunting lodge. Over the next 400 years the buildings became decayed, eventually being purchased in 1933 by Stephen Courtauld, a member of the wealthy textile family, who began to restore the Great Hall and construct a new wing in the prevailing Art Deco style. Eltham Palace became a fashionable venue for weekend parties until the Second World War.

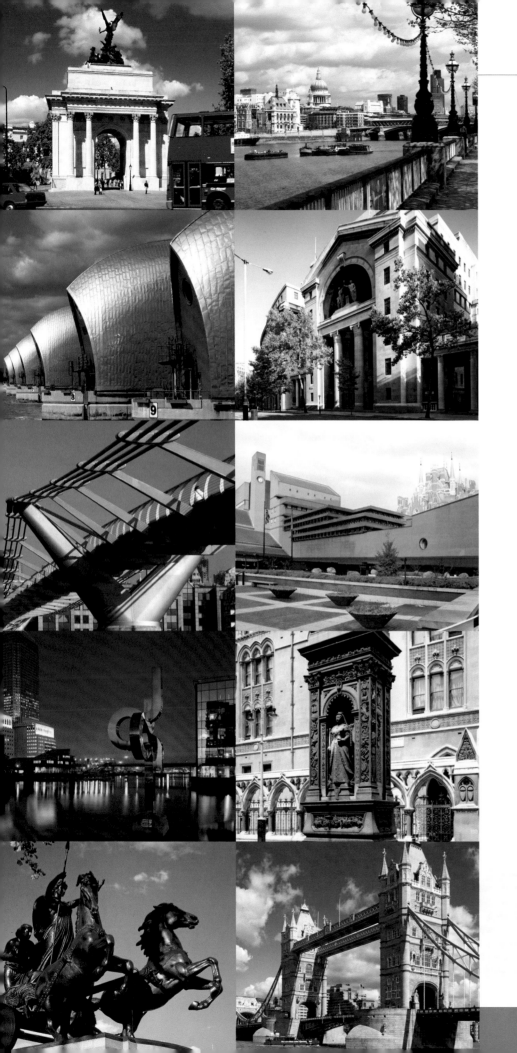

# London Landmarks

POSSIBLY THE MOST FAMOUS ASPECT OF LONDON IS ITS SKYLINE, WITH ITS QUIRKY SHAPES SILHOUETTING BUILDINGS THAT SPAN THE LAST MILLENNIUM. HOWEVER, MANY OTHERS ARE EQUALLY ICONIC EVEN IF RELATIVELY DIMINUTIVE IN STATURE, SUCH AS THE STATUE OF EROS IN PICCADILLY CIRCUS, AND MARBLE ARCH ON THE CORNER OF HYDE PARK. MOST PEOPLE WILL BE FAMILIAR WITH LANDMARKS SUCH AS BIG BEN, BUT OTHERS WILL BE A REVELATION, SUCH AS THE TEMPLE BAR MONUMENT AT THE BOUNDARY OF THE CITIES OF LONDON AND WESTMINSTER.

Some of these landmarks, such as Southwark Cathedral, date back centuries, while others, for example the London Eye, were created for the twenty-first century. Perhaps the most striking feature of London, particularly when seeing it for the first time, is the strange juxtaposition of buildings – ancient churches and modern glass skyscrapers vying for the viewer's attention. Many of these buildings were created at the height of Empire, when London wanted to proclaim to the world how magnificent and wealthy it was. However, the engineers and architects of today have continued in the same vein by creating some of the most innovative and exciting buildings and structural landmarks of their own.

# Harrods

## KENSINGTON AND CHELSEA

Arguably the most famous store in the world, Harrods was founded by Charles Henry Harrod (1799–1885) in 1824. In 1849 he made the decision to move his business to its present location to capitalize on the trade that would follow the Great Exhibition two years later. The store was rebuilt as you see it today after a disastrous fire in 1883. The Harrods motto is *Omnia Omnibus Ubique*, which means 'all things for all people, everywhere'. Among its clients over the years have been Oscar Wilde, Charlie Chaplin and several members of the Royal Family.

# Albert Memorial at Kensington Gardens

## KENSINGTON AND CHELSEA

Queen Victoria opened this memorial to her husband Prince Albert (1819–61), who died at the age of only 42 of typhoid, which he contracted at Windsor Castle. The monument, by Sir George Gilbert Scott (1811–78), is in the Gothic Revival style and is essentially an ornate ciborium (a canopy-like structure) under which Albert sits, holding a catalogue of the Great Exhibition of 1851 that he had helped create. Around the base of the monument is the Frieze of Parnassus, depicting famous painters, sculptors, architects, musicians and poets.

# Wellington Arch

## CITY OF WESTMINSTER

This triumphal arch was completed in 1830 as a monument to the British victories in the Napoleonic Wars, most notably those of the Duke of Wellington at Waterloo in 1815. The figure on top is the winged angel of peace calming the horses of war. Originally it was an enormous equestrian statue of Wellington, the largest of its type ever made, which was removed to Aldershot after the Duke died. The arch stands opposite Apsley House at Hyde Park Corner, and the public can use a staircase inside to reach the viewing balcony just below the statue.

# Piccadilly Circus
## CITY OF WESTMINSTER

A favourite meeting place for visitors to London, Piccadilly Circus was created in 1819 to link Piccadilly with the newly created Regent Street. In the 1880s the newly created Shaftesbury Avenue terminated here, creating a busy thoroughfare. At the centre of this circular junction (circus) is the Shaftesbury memorial fountain (more commonly referred to as Eros), installed in 1893 and one of the first to be cast in aluminium. The illuminated signs were installed here as early as 1910, just four years after the Underground station was opened.

# Admiralty Arch
## CITY OF WESTMINSTER

Admiralty Arch was created in 1912 as the gateway for a processional route along The Mall towards Buckingham Palace, and takes its name from the adjoining government buildings. The arch contains government offices as well as a residence for the First Sea Lord. King Edward VII (1841–1910) commissioned the work in memory of his mother Queen Victoria, whose long reign ended in 1901, although he did not live long enough to see it unveiled. In front of Admiralty Arch is a statue of Captain James Cook (1728–79), the British explorer and navigator.

# Trafalgar Square

## CITY OF WESTMINSTER

The church of St Martin in the Fields, which dominates the centre of this picture, was built in 1726, its name suggested by the topography of this era. At this time there was also an equestrian statue of King Charles I, which still survives, on the south side of the square (not shown), which today marks the geographical centre of London. Sir Charles Barry (1795–1860), the architect of the new Houses of Parliament, laid out Trafalgar Square in the 1840s incorporating the National Gallery (shown on the left).

# Nelson's Column

## CITY OF WESTMINSTER

The most prominent feature of Trafalgar Square is the column erected to commemorate the victories of Horatio, Lord Nelson (1758–1805), most notably at Trafalgar in October 1805. Nelson had been given a state funeral at St Paul's Cathedral, such was his status as the naval hero who defeated the combined navies of France and Spain during the Napoleonic Wars. The four bronze plaques at the base of the column depict these victories and were cast from cannons that had been captured from the enemy.

# Bush House

## CITY OF WESTMINSTER

In the early 1900s as part of a slum clearance scheme, the Aldwych area of London was improved with a new road called Kingsway, one of the widest in London, which opens out into a D-shaped thoroughfare containing a series of elegant buildings, such as Australia House and the Waldorf Hotel. Facing Kingsway is Bush House, named after the American businessman Irving T. Bush (1869–1948), who financed this building intended as a commercial centre. In the event it was occupied until recently by the BBC World Service.

# St Clement Danes Church

## CITY OF WESTMINSTER

On an island in the centre of The Strand stands the church of St Clement Danes. The church fell victim to the Blitz in the Second World War, but was refurbished and dedicated to the Royal Air Force. Over the doorway is an inscription that reads 'Built by Christopher Wren 1682. Destroyed by the thunderbolts of air warfare 1941. Restored by the RAF 1958.' Outside the church are statues of two RAF wartime leaders, Air Chief Marshall Lord Dowding (1882–1970) and Marshal of the Royal Air Force Sir Arthur Harris (1892–1984).

# Cleopatra's Needle

## CITY OF WESTMINSTER

Cleopatra's Needle is located along the north Embankment of the River Thames, having arrived there in 1879. The obelisk dates from about 1400 BC, when it was quarried, cut and engraved with dedications to the Pharaoh Thutmose III and later Rameses II, and then Cleopatra. It was given to Britain as a gift from the Viceroy of Egypt, Muhammad Ali (1769–1849), in 1819, to commemorate British victories against the French in the Napoleonic Wars. The delay in installation was due to the engineering difficulties encountered in moving an object weighing over 200 tons.

# Embankment Place

## CITY OF WESTMINSTER

This striking postmodern building is by Terry Farrell and Partners and opened in 1990. The structure was built to replace the canopy for trains arriving at Charing Cross Station that had partially collapsed in 1906 and not been replaced. Farrell's design removed the remains of the old canopy and replaced it with this very distinctive double canopy. Beneath and on either side of the canopies are office blocks integrated into the design, making use of the air rights. On the ground floor are retail units.

# Big Ben
## CITY OF WESTMINSTER

The correct name for this building is the Westminster Clock Tower. The 13-ton bell that chimes the hour, situated in the housing above the clock faces, is called Big Ben, possibly named after Benjamin Hall (1802–67), who oversaw its installation. Today the entire structure is affectionately known as Big Ben and is probably the most iconic of all London landmarks. The tower, which forms part of the Palace of Westminster, is made of brick in the lower part and cast iron in the upper, with a limestone finish to match the other buildings.

# Boudicca Statue
## CITY OF WESTMINSTER

Queen Boudicca was the leader of the Iceni tribe during the early years of the Roman occupation in Britain. Despite her husband appeasing the occupying army, when he died the Romans refused to allow his daughters to inherit his small kingdom as specified in his will. Instead they took the Iceni estates by force and subjected the daughters to a brutal attack. Boudicca responded by establishing a small army and destroying the Roman settlements, including those in London. The dynamic sculpture at the end of Westminster Bridge encapsulates the ferocity of her rebellion.

# Westminster Abbey

## CITY OF WESTMINSTER

The two towers of the west entrance are the building's most recent additions. Most of the current structure was erected in the thirteenth century, when the earlier church from the eleventh century was demolished to accommodate it. Between them, the two churches have witnessed every coronation in England since 1066. The current church is known as a Royal Peculiar, one of only three churches that falls under the jurisdiction of the monarch rather than a bishop, and has been used for most royal weddings in the twentieth century.

# Westminster Cathedral

## CITY OF WESTMINSTER

The Roman Catholic cathedral in Westminster was created in the early years of the twentieth century and, rather unusually, built in a pseudo-Byzantine style. It is the largest Catholic church in England and has been visited by two Popes, John Paul II (1920–2005) and Benedict XVI (b. 1927), who both celebrated Mass there. Her Majesty the Queen also visited the cathedral in 1977, on the occasion of her Silver Jubilee. The most striking feature is its campanile (bell tower), which towers some 87 metres above the building.

# Marble Arch

## CITY OF WESTMINSTER

Originally a triumphal edifice at the front of Buckingham Palace, the Marble Arch was moved to its present location in 1851, when a new façade was added to the palace enclosing its courtyard. It was intended that a statue of King George IV should be placed on the top, which was eventually sited in Trafalgar Square. Despite being moved from Buckingham Palace, vehicles can still not drive through the arch in its present location, apart from members of the Royal Family. The small rooms inside the arch were used as a police station until it was decommissioned in 1950.

# British Library

## CAMDEN

A controversial building at the time of its design, it took 30 years to complete, referred to by the architect Colin St John Wilson (1922–2007) as the "30 years' war", due to the political wrangling and economic difficulties that surrounded it. This state-of-the-art building is the largest of its kind in the world and holds about 14 million books, as well as priceless manuscripts, including two copies of the Magna Carta, Charlotte Bronte's *Jane Eyre*, Chaucer's *Canterbury Tales*, the *Lindisfarne Gospels* and a copy of the *Gutenberg Bible*.

# Battersea Power Station

## WANDSWORTH

Decommissioned as a power station in 1983, it is a prominent feature of the London skyline and has made numerous cultural appearances, including in The Beatles' film *Help* and as an album cover for the rock band Pink Floyd. Since its closure, numerous schemes have been proposed for the Grade II-listed building, including a theme park and a shopping mall, but the present owners who purchased the site in 2006 have proposed a new housing development and the re-use of the power station fuelled by biomass and waste.

# SIS Building

## LAMBETH

This distinctive 'Aztec' temple by the architect Terry Farrell is for the use of the Secret Intelligence Services, formerly MI6. The building is also referred to as 'Legoland' and was originally built speculatively until purchased by Margaret Thatcher's government in 1988. The building has appeared in several Bond films, most notably in the opening sequence of *The World is Not Enough*, when the hero emerges from the front of the building in a powerboat, in order to chase an assassin along the Thames.

# South Bank Lion

## LAMBETH

Made from a ceramic composite called Coadestone, this lion once featured as one of a pair outside a brewery close to its present location at the south bank of Westminster Bridge. The material was developed in the 1770s by Mrs Eleanor Coade (1733–1821), who manufactured a number of decorative ornaments that could be produced more economically, and would weather better, than carved stone. It was so successful that a royal warrant was granted and the material used for decorative ornament at Buckingham Palace, the Royal Pavilion in Brighton, and the Royal Naval College, Greenwich.

# London Eye

## LAMBETH

Designed as an attraction to celebrate the arrival of the millennium in 2000, the observation wheel known as the London Eye was intended to be on site for one year only. Its popularity, however, determined otherwise and the attraction still draws large crowds and provides a striking feature on the London skyline, particularly at night when it is illuminated in different colours. On New Year's Eve and other occasions, the fireworks display along this part of the River Thames creates a wheel-shaped silhouette.

# City of London from the South Bank

## LAMBETH

When St Paul's Cathedral was completed in 1710, it was the tallest building in London. Today its dome still stands tall in the city skyline despite being dwarfed by taller buildings behind it. Legislation is in place to safeguard some views of St Paul's from being obscured by new structures, in order to preserve its majesty. During the Blitz in 1940–41, when nearly 80 per cent of the buildings in the City of London were destroyed, it was the cathedral that remained defiant against enemy bombing, a beacon of hope in Britain's 'darkest hour'.

# Temple Bar Memorial

## CITY OF LONDON

In a tradition dating back to the reign of Elizabeth I, when the sovereign wishes to enter the City of London, the Lord Mayor of London meets them at the Temple Bar gate and offers a sword of state as a mark of loyalty to the Crown. The statue in the middle of the road replaced the gateway that once stood at the entrance, and there is a frieze on the replacement depicting Queen Elizabeth I and the royal procession meeting the Lord Mayor.

# St Bride's Church

## CITY OF LONDON

After St Paul's Cathedral, St Bride's is the tallest church in the City of London. Designed by Sir Christopher Wren to replace the original church destroyed in the Great Fire of London in 1666, it is a prominent feature of the City skyline. Its unusual steeple is said to have inspired the making of the first tiered wedding cake. There are many associations with the church, including the diarist Samuel Pepys (1633–1703), who was baptized here, and the 'father of the English clock', Thomas Tompion (1639–1713), who was a parishioner.

# St Paul's Cathedral

## CITY OF LONDON

When Sir Christopher Wren was planning the new cathedral following the Great Fire of London, he was mapping the layout using some of the rubble from the old cathedral as markers. One of these stones had the Latin word *Resurgum* (I will rise again) carved into it, which provided a stimulus for Wren's new design. In a pediment above the south door to the new cathedral, Wren had this word carved into the stone and above it he placed an ornate figure of a phoenix.

# High Altar at St Paul's Cathedral

## CITY OF LONDON

Wren apparently decided to decorate the inside of the dome of St Paul's with mosaics, which were never completed. In stark contrast to his plain Baroque design at the west end of the cathedral, the east end is sumptuously decorated with gold and coloured mosaics. The decision to alter Wren's masterpiece was taken in the nineteenth century, when Queen Victoria complained about its plainness. A number of celebrated artists and designers were commissioned over various stages, the most recent being completed in the early twentieth century.

# Millennium Bridge

## CITY OF LONDON

Created as part of the millennium celebrations in 2000, the footbridge links the Tate Modern gallery, which opened in the same year, and the southern approach to St Paul's Cathedral. Within two weeks of the bridge opening, however, it was forced to close for safety reasons and was not re-opened until two years later. The bridge featured in two of the Harry Potter films: *The Order of the Phoenix*, when Harry and his friends fly above the Thames on broomsticks; and *The Half Blood Prince*, when it was destroyed by the 'death-eaters'.

# Bank of England and Royal Exchange

## CITY OF LONDON

One of the busiest junctions in London is the intersection of the Bank of England and the Royal Exchange in the City. The Bank of England, shown on the left, was established in 1694, but the present building was not erected until nearly 100 years later. Completed in 1833, the external wall is all that is left of the original plan, as it was substantially rebuilt in the 1930s. The present Royal Exchange was completed in 1844 as a trading centre, but is now used as a fashionable shopping mall.

# Gherkin

## CITY OF LONDON

This iconic building with its distinctive shape can be seen punctuating the London skyline from a number of different vantage points. Here it is seen juxtaposed in stark contrast with a sixteenth-century church that managed to escape damage in both the Great Fire of 1666 and the Blitz of 1940–41. The post-modern energy-efficient building by Lord Foster (b. 1935) is officially called 30 St Mary Axe (its address), or the Swiss-Re building, but due to its shape it is better known as the Gherkin.

# Lloyd's Building

## CITY OF LONDON

Almost opposite the Gherkin is the earlier Lloyd's Building by Lord Rogers (b. 1933). Completed in 1986, it features a trademark of Rogers' design in the placing of service ducts, lifts and utilities outside of the building to maximize the use of internal space. He and Foster gained a reputation for creating so-called 'hi-tech' architecture at the end of the twentieth century. Like most of Rogers' buildings, it looks unusual during the day but spectacular at night, with quirky lighting schemes revealing internal spaces.

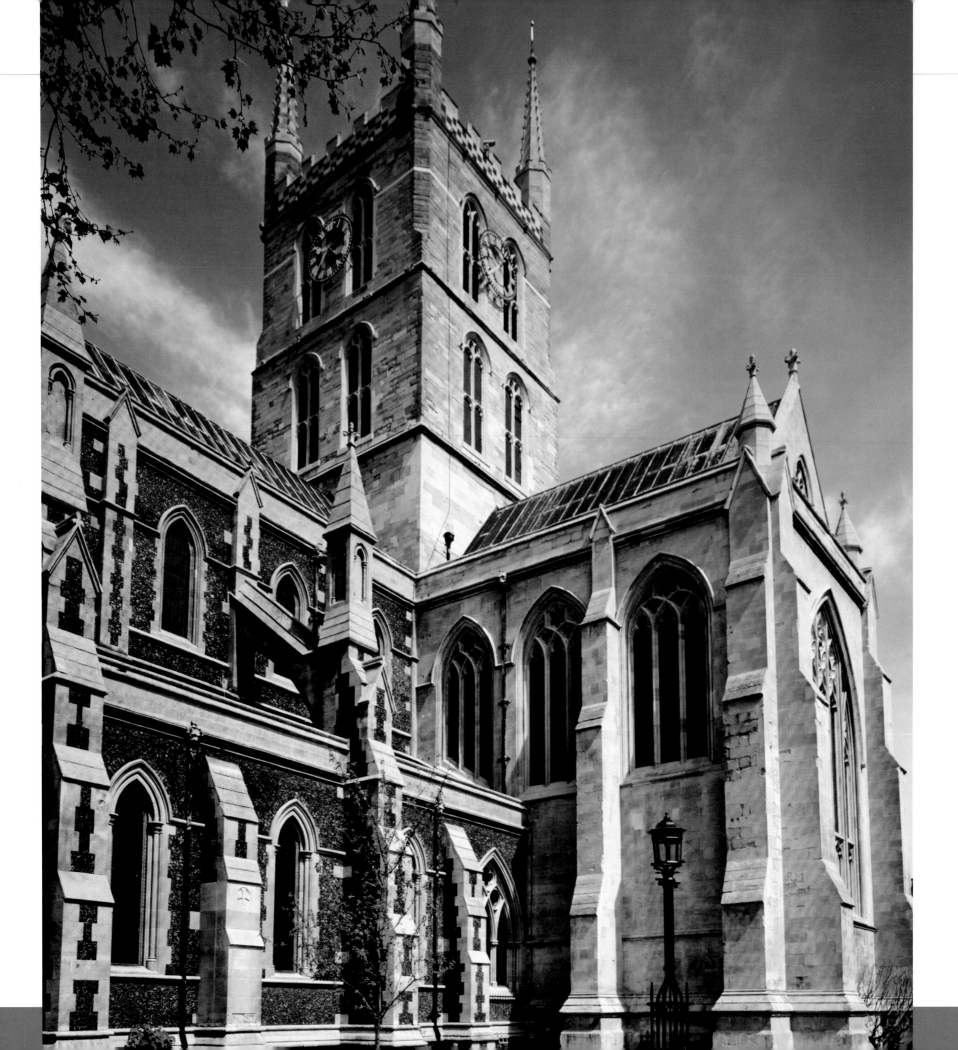

# Southwark Cathedral

## SOUTHWARK

There has been a church on this site since at least the twelfth century, although the present building dates from the thirteenth, having been rebuilt after a fire. Until 1905 it was the parish church of St Saviours, but a new diocese was created for Southwark and it was designated as its cathedral. It has many historical connections, being the burial place of William Shakespeare's brother Edmund (1580–1607) and the site of the baptism of John Harvard (1607–38), the founder of the college that bears his name.

# City Hall

## SOUTHWARK

This striking building was created in 2002 as the administrative headquarters of the Greater London Authority and its CEO, the Mayor of London, together with the London Assembly. It was built two years after the Greater London Authority was created following the dissolution of the previous governing body, the Greater London Council, in 1986. The building, by Lord Foster, is essentially glass and symbolizes transparency in government, but its unusual shape has prompted the use of pejorative descriptions such as the 'glass testicle' by the first mayor to occupy its offices, Ken Livingstone (b. 1945).

# Tower Bridge
## TOWER HAMLETS

Possibly the most photographed and easily recognized landmark in London is Tower Bridge, the most easterly of the bridges on the Thames. It was opened to provide a gateway for large ships coming into the Pool of London in 1894. The bridge is part-suspension and part-bascule (drawbridge) design, its frame made of iron and then covered in stone to resemble its close neighbour, the Tower of London. The bridge still opens on average three times per day for tall ships.

This is an official London Sightseeing boat

# Canary Wharf

## TOWER HAMLETS

This 'mini-Manhattan' area of London is a business district and takes its name from the dockland wharf that once occupied this site for the unloading of produce from the Canary Islands. With the advent of containerization in the 1960s, the whole of the Docklands area, some eight square miles, eventually closed down and relocated to a deeper area of the Thames at Tilbury. The area lay empty until the 1980s, when government money funded an enterprise zone at Canary Wharf. Today, there are about 90,000 people employed in this commercial district.

# Cabot Square at Canary Wharf

## TOWER HAMLETS

The first major development at Canary Wharf was the creation of Cabot Square, and the first offices to be opened were those of Credit Suisse, who wanted it as a 'back office'. However the prestigious One Canada Square (shown in the centre of the picture) was built at the same time and became a symbol of the regeneration of the area. Soon after, other companies such as Morgan Stanley opened offices at this location, leading to HSBC bank locating their world headquarters here. Below the piazza is a shopping mall with over 200 shops and restaurants.

# Olympic Stadium

## NEWHAM

A new Olympic stadium has been created to host the 2012 London Olympic and Paralympic Games. This 80,000-seat stadium, which will be used for all the athletic events plus the opening and closing ceremonies, is a part-permanent and part-temporary structure, in line with the bid promise to create the greenest games ever staged. The upper tiers are temporary and after the games the stadium will be reduced to 25,000 seats. In its construction the stadium used recycled materials and a low-carbon concrete mix using industrial waste.

# Thames Barrier

## GREENWICH

In January 1953 much of the east coast of England was flooded due to a freak storm and an exceptionally high tide that killed over 300 people and made many thousands homeless. The building of a flood barrier was not feasible until the London docks relocated to Tilbury because of the need for large ships to gain access. With the relocation completed, construction began in 1974 and was finished 10 years later. It has been activated over 100 times since, when high tides and storm surges threaten the coastline and the River Thames estuary.

# London Parks & Gardens

THE GREEN SPACES OF THE CAPITAL ARE OFTEN REFERRED TO AS THE 'LUNGS OF LONDON', PROVIDING A HOME FOR MOST OF THE SEVEN MILLION TREES IN THE CITY. APART FROM THE ROYAL PARKS THERE ARE A NUMBER OF FORESTED AREAS SUCH AS EPPING FOREST, AND OPEN, LESS FORMALIZED PARKLANDS SUCH AS WIMBLEDON COMMON. LONDON IS ALSO FAMED FOR ITS RESIDENTIAL 'SQUARES', A TRADITION THAT BEGAN IN THE EARLY EIGHTEENTH CENTURY AS THE CITY EXPANDED ITS POPULATION AND BECAME MORE PROSPEROUS.

In 1715 the population of London was about 600,000 and by 1801 it had risen to over one million. By the end of that century the population had more than quadrupled in the wake of increased commercial activities, the Industrial Revolution and a burgeoning Empire. The need for more housing was matched by the creation of new green spaces such as Battersea Park in South London and Victoria Park in the east. The process continues today with the creation of the first major landscaped park in over 150 years on the site of the Olympic Games complex, which in legacy will become the Queen Elizabeth Olympic Park.

# Deer in Richmond Park

## RICHMOND

The largest of the parks in London, Richmond is a Site of Special Scientific Interest and a National Reserve, comprising nearly 2,500 acres of open fields and woodland. King Charles I enclosed the park as a hunting ground, but after the English Civil War it was reclaimed for the people. Now it is in the care of the Royal Parks. There are two species of deer in the park, red and fallow deer, totalling about 600. From the highest point, King Henry VIII's Mound, there is a view to St Paul's Cathedral that is protected by statute.

# Kew Gardens

## RICHMOND

Although more commonly known as Kew Gardens, its official title is the Royal Botanic Gardens, and it was designated a World Heritage Site by UNESCO in 2003. It is effectively a 300-acre site that combines a pleasure garden and a botanical science centre. It began in the eighteenth century when Frederick, Prince of Wales (1707–51) began developing the pleasure garden, a scheme that was continued by his wife Princess Augusta (1719–72) after his premature death. The most significant changes came later in the century with the landscaping by Lancelot 'Capability' Brown (1716–83).

# Palm House
# in Kew Gardens

## RICHMOND

The Palm House was designed by Decimus Burton (1800–81) and built by the engineer Richard Turner (1798–1881) between 1844 and 1848. This cathedral-like structure is made of iron and glass, some of which is curved, and is probably the most significant of the great Victorian buildings of its type to survive. In this era it was fashionable to collect exotic species from overseas, and the construction of this building facilitated the keeping and cultivation of various species for the public to see and enjoy.

# Treetop Walkway in Kew Gardens

## RICHMOND

One of the best ways to see the trees at Kew Gardens is to use the Treetop Walkway that stands 18 metres above ground. Marks Barfield and Partners, who also created the London Eye, designed the scheme, which opened in 2008, to carefully blend with the environment so as to be as unobtrusive as possible. The structure is based on the Fibonacci numerical sequence, something that is present in many living organisms. Apart from inspecting the oak and chestnut tree crowns, there is also ample opportunity to see wildlife.

# Temperate House in Kew Gardens

## RICHMOND

Begun in 1860 but not completed until 1898, this is the largest surviving Victorian greenhouse in the world, covering in excess of 50,000 square feet. Decimus Burton, who did not live long enough to see its completion, designed the Temperate House to accommodate the great number and variety of species brought back by the plant collectors. Many plants that have grown elsewhere at Kew are transferred here, the most notable being the Chilean Wine Palm, which is almost 60 feet in height. It is also home to some of the rarest and most endangered plant species in the world.

# Kyoto Garden in Holland Park

### KENSINGTON AND CHELSEA

Holland Park is a mix of woodland and public recreational areas that include tennis courts and a cricket pitch. It also contains the ruins of Holland House, once a majestic stately home frequented by the Royal Family, which was destroyed in the Blitz. It was after the Second World War that the gardens were opened to the public. The Kyoto Garden, a traditional Japanese design, was opened in 1991 to celebrate the Japan Festival in London the following year, sponsored and funded by the Kyoto Chamber of Commerce.

# Sunken Garden at Kensington Palace

### KENSINGTON AND CHELSEA

Unlike the asymmetrical English cottage garden, the Sunken Garden at Kensington Palace is Dutch in origin and is mainly geometrical in design. Plant borders are regular and are usually interspersed with rectangular or circular water features. Dutchman William of Orange, who became William III of England in 1688, had the palace built, and his wife, the joint ruler Mary II, created the gardens. Queen Caroline (1683–1737), consort to George II, continued the work in the eighteenth century with great enthusiasm and energy.

# Italian Gardens in Kensington Gardens

## KENSINGTON AND CHELSEA

In 1730 Queen Caroline ordered the damming of the River Westbourne at the head of Kensington Gardens to create a lake now known as the Serpentine, due to its winding shape. This part of the lake is known as the Long Water and at its head is the Italian Gardens, whose fountains are fed by the river. These elaborate and formal gardens have been used as locations in various films, most notably in *Bridget Jones – Edge of Reason*, made in 2004, in which the two male protagonists have a fight and end up in the fountain.

# Hyde Park

## CITY OF WESTMINSTER

In 1851, Hyde Park was used as the site of the Crystal Palace for the Great Exhibition, incorporating some of the trees already growing there. Since then the park has been the focus for many other events, including rock concerts; the most notable was staged by the Rolling Stones in 1969 and attracted crowds of over a quarter of a million people. At the north-east edge of the park is Speakers' Corner, where anyone can exercise their right to speak on any subject, providing it is lawful, non-abusive and does not incite hatred.

# Rotten Row
# in Hyde Park

## CITY OF WESTMINSTER

When King William III moved his court to Kensington Palace, he established a road inside Hyde Park that became known as the *Rue* or *Route de Roi*, intended as a safe route for him to and from St James's Palace. It became a very fashionable place for high society to see and be seen until the 1870s, when it was converted to a sand track for horses and their riders. Today it is known as 'Rotten Row' (a corruption of the original French), but still used for that purpose, most notably by the Household Cavalry whose barracks are close by.

# Serpentine in Hyde Park

## CITY OF WESTMINSTER

The Serpentine Lake was created in the eighteenth century by damming up the River Westbourne, which used to flow through Hyde Park into the Thames. Today this has been reversed, the lake filled by pumping water from the river. The lake provides amenities such as boating in the summer months, and is where the Lansbury Lido is located for swimming. Members of the swimming club compete in an annual race on Christmas Day. In 2012 the lake will host the Olympic open-water marathon event and the swimming leg of the triathlon.

# Serpentine Bridge in Hyde Park

## CITY OF WESTMINSTER

The bridge across the Serpentine is part of the West Carriage Drive dividing Hyde Park and Kensington Gardens. It was designed and built by John Rennie Jr (1794–1874), whose father, John Sr, designed the old London Bridge that is now located at Lake Havasu City in Arizona. The Serpentine Bridge is a very similar design to the old London Bridge, which was completed by Rennie Jr after his father's death in 1821. The bridge is a favourite spot in the summer to view the activities along the lake.

# Royal Gun Salute at Green Park

## CITY OF WESTMINSTER

The King's Troop, Royal Horse Artillery provides the gun salutes at Green Park and other locations in London on state occasions. Traditionally the salute at Green Park and Hyde Park is a 41-gun salvo for the State Opening of Parliament and for official visits by foreign heads of state, both of which take place at Green Park. On other occasions, such as the Queen's birthday and Coronation Day, the salute is of 62 guns and is fired from Hyde Park. There is also a salute at the Tower of London by the same unit.

# Canada Gate at Green Park

## CITY OF WESTMINSTER

The gate was presented to London by Canada as its contribution to the processional route of The Mall which was laid out in the early part of the twentieth century by Sir Aston Webb (1849–1930). In the scheme, Webb created Admiralty Arch and re-surfaced the front of Buckingham Palace, with other Commonwealth countries such as Australia and South Africa providing its gates. Behind the Canada Gate is a memorial to Canadian servicemen who died in the two World Wars, opened in 1994. The pattern on the memorial utilizes the symbol of Canada, the maple leaf.

# Daffodils in St James's Park

## CITY OF WESTMINSTER

St James's Park is the oldest of the Royal Parks in London, taking its name from the Hospital of St James for lepers, converted in the sixteenth century to St James's Palace. The park was created by Henry VIII as a tilt yard (courtyard for jousting) and bowling alley. In 1649 King Charles I was escorted across the park from the palace to his place of execution in Whitehall. The park was sadly neglected until 1814, when the Prince Regent held a gala here to celebrate the centenary of the Hanoverian dynasty in England.

# Lake in St James's Park

## CITY OF WESTMINSTER

Following the neglect of the Commonwealth years of the 1650s, King Charles II (1630–85) laid out the new enlarged park, merging the existing Rosamund's Pond with a new canal to create a long stretch of water that was filled with livestock, including a gift of two pelicans from the Russian Ambassador. The lake and park were substantially altered in the eighteenth and nineteenth centuries with the addition of gas lighting in 1822 and an iron suspension bridge (since replaced). The present bridge affords a view towards Buckingham Palace framed by trees.

# Crocuses in St James's Park

## CITY OF WESTMINSTER

In all seasons, St James's Park is always colourful. The spring provides a 'host of golden daffodils' as well as beds of tulips and camellia shrubs. The early summer is resplendent with azaleas and rhododendrons, and later there are dahlias in many of the borders. The autumn relies on the changing colours of the hundreds of trees in the park, and in the winter there are carpets of crocuses. Adding to the colour, the lake is home to over 25 bird species, including ducks and geese.

# Duck Island Cottage in St James's Park

## CITY OF WESTMINSTER

At the eastern end of the lake is Duck Island, named after the waterfowl that use the land. On the island is a small cottage, created in 1841 as a lodge for the Ornithological Society. There was also accommodation for the park keeper. The roof of the house provided two dovecotes and inside the cottage was a steam-powered hatching device to provide artificial incubation for wildfowl, an apparatus that was developed in the 1820s. The cottage was restored in 1982, including the waterway that originally ran beneath.

# Victoria Tower Gardens

## CITY OF WESTMINSTER

These gardens to the south of the Victoria Tower of the Houses of Parliament (shown in the centre) were created in the nineteenth century as a recreational area, part of the Thames Embankment system. There are a number of features in this park, including the Buxton Memorial, a neo-Gothic drinking fountain that commemorates the abolition of slavery in 1834. The Member of Parliament Charles Buxton (1823–71) commissioned it to honour his father and other abolitionists such as William Wilberforce (1759–1833). The memorial was made in 1865.

# Statue in Victoria Tower Gardens

## CITY OF WESTMINSTER

The British government purchased this *Burghers of Calais* sculpture by Auguste Rodin in 1911. The casting is one of 12; the first, made in 1895, is in Calais. After Edward III of England had defeated the French at the Battle of Crécy in 1346, he laid siege to the town of Calais, telling the citizens he would spare their lives if they surrendered six of the town's elders for execution. His wife Phillipa of Hainault (1314–69) intervened and pleaded with the king to spare their lives. It is this scene that Rodin captured with magnificent pathos.

# Regent's Park

## CITY OF WESTMINSTER/CAMDEN

Claimed by Henry VIII from the monastery that once owned the land, Regent's Park remains one of the Royal Parks. Its name is taken from the Prince Regent, who planned to build a summer palace here together with a boulevard of shops stretching from his home at Carlton House to the park. To fund this venture his architect John Nash proposed the speculative building of 56 villas. In the event the boulevard, Regent St, was built, together with some of the villas, but the palace was never realized.

# London Zoo in Regent's Park

## CITY OF WESTMINSTER/CAMDEN

Prior to the opening of the zoo in Regent's Park the only place in London where exotic animals were kept and could be seen was at the Tower of London, where a Royal menagerie had been kept for over 600 years. Although the new zoo was created in 1828 it was not open to the public until 1847. The zoo is a scientific research centre as well as being a public attraction, and today has over 700 different species of animal. One of the most popular attractions is the Gorilla Kingdom, opened in 2007.

# Hampstead Heath

## CAMDEN

Artists such as John Constable (1775–1837) and Ford Madox Brown (1821–93), and writers such as Charles Dickens have immortalized the views from Hampstead Heath, the highest point in London. Although it lies within the Borough of Camden, the City of London Corporation is responsible for its upkeep. There are many attractions on the Heath, including Jack Straw's Castle, an old coaching inn dating from 1721 and named after one of the leaders of the Peasants Revolt in 1381 (the peasants met at Hampstead Heath before confronting the King).

# Royal Observatory in Greenwich Park

## GREENWICH

From this viewpoint in Greenwich Park one can see the Royal Observatory perched high on the hill once occupied by Duke Humphrey's Tower in the fifteenth century. In 1619 King James I enclosed Greenwich Park with a brick wall that is still visible and marks the southern boundary. Many of the trees planted in that period survive. The park was originally only open to the public on certain days including Bank Holidays, and it was common for children to 'tumble' down the steep hill for fun.

# Greenwich Park towards the Docklands

## GREENWICH

One of the most spectacular views across London is from the top of Greenwich Park. In the foreground are the Queen's House and the former Royal Naval College this side of the River Thames. It was here that Sir Francis Chichester (1901–72), disembarked from his yacht *Gypsy Moth IV* to be knighted by the Queen following his single-handed circumnavigation of the globe in 1967. The Queen used the same sword that had been used by her predecessor Elizabeth I when knighting Sir Francis Drake in 1579.

# London Transport

ONE OF LONDON'S SUCCESS STORIES, AND THE ENVY OF MANY OTHER CITIES, IS ITS PUBLIC TRANSPORT SYSTEM. THIS IS HARDLY SURPRISING SINCE RAILWAY TECHNOLOGY BEGAN IN BRITAIN. LONDON CREATED THE FIRST UNDERGROUND RAILWAY NETWORK IN 1867 AND WAS THE FIRST TO ELECTRIFY THE SYSTEM IN 1890. STARTING IN 1829, AND REGULATED BY 1855, A COMMON SIGHT ON THE STREETS OF LONDON WAS THE HORSE-DRAWN OMNIBUS, WITH MOTORBUSES SUCCEEDING THEM FROM 1906.

Trains and buses came together in the 1930s as the London Passenger Transport Board (LPTB), unifying and co-ordinating a public transport infrastructure that is still in place today, organized by Transport for London (TfL), a body directly under the control of the Mayor's office.

The brief is much larger for TfL than it was for the LPTB, as there is a larger underground network that now includes the Docklands Light Railway. Additionally TfL is also responsible for policing the licensed taxicab and mini-cab trades. In new initiatives they have also developed the Barclays Bank sponsored cycle hire facility in London and are also keen to promote other modes of public transport such as waterbuses.

# Victoria Station

## CITY OF WESTMINSTER

Originally two separate termini for different rail companies, Victoria Station was created after the companies merged in 1899. The station services trains to Brighton and the south coast, the line being the first to cross the River Thames. The station became popular when the first day-trippers visited the south coast in the nineteenth century and later when boat trains were used to cross the English Channel to the continent, an event brought into sharp focus during the First World War.

# Westminster Underground Station
## CITY OF WESTMINSTER

The newly refurbished Westminster Station was opened in 1999 to accommodate the new Jubilee Line extension, deep below the existing station that previously only facilitated the District and Circle lines. It was decided to include Westminster, as the Jubilee Line had to be extended east to handle the increased commuter traffic to Docklands. The shaft was excavated to a depth of 130 feet, making it the deepest station in central London. Above the station is the iconic, but controversial, Portcullis House, designed by the same architects as Westminster Station.

# No. 9 Bus to Aldwych
## CITY OF WESTMINSTER

The vehicle shown here is one of the old Routemaster buses that ran in London between 1958 and 2005, when they were withdrawn on the orders of the Mayor of London. There were nearly 3,000 made but only about 1,000 of them survive today. However, many of those survivors are still running, including several used as public transport on so-called 'heritage routes'. Another common sight is for them to be used as wedding vehicles, transporting guests from the ceremony to the reception. A new version of the bus is now planned for the capital.

PUBLIC
UNDERGROUND
SUBWAY
Bakerloo line
Piccadilly line
Travel information

# Piccadilly Circus
# Underground Station

## CITY OF WESTMINSTER

This station was the first to be built entirely underground with access only via a staircase. Like the original road plan above, the station is circular in design and was created by the doyen of London transport architects, Charles Holden (1875–1960), in 1925. The original station was opened in 1906 and, like most stations, had its ticket office at street level. At this time there were about 1.5 million passengers per year but by 1922 this had increased to 18 million, hence the reason to build a new booking hall that would improve passenger flow.

# Taxis on
# New Bond Street

## CITY OF WESTMINSTER

The official name for the taxicab is the Hackney Carriage, which was originally a horse-drawn conveyance dating back to the seventeenth century. The modern conveyance is of course motorized and manufactured by LTI in Coventry, England. The vehicles are registered within a division of TfL to maintain their roadworthiness. Additionally taxi drivers have to take an examination called 'the Knowledge', in which they are expected to demonstrate a mastery of destinations and routes in London. Typically the Knowledge takes about three years to complete and usually requires many attempts to pass.

# Paddington Station

## CITY OF WESTMINSTER

Designed by one of England's greatest engineers, Isambard Kingdom Brunel (1806–59), this station gained still further fame through the children's stories of Paddington Bear by Michael Bond (b. 1926). The station is the London terminus for trains from the west of England and much of Wales, the route originally known as the Great Western Railway and also designed by Brunel. Probably the most famous locomotive of the great steam age that ran the route from Paddington to Exeter was *The Flying Dutchman*.

# St Pancras Station

## CAMDEN

The building shown here, which featured in two of the Harry Potter films, is in fact the St Pancras Renaissance Hotel that fronts St Pancras station. When the station was opened in 1868 the train sheds, designed by William Barlow (1812–1902), had the largest single-span roof in the world. Sir George Gilbert Scott designed the hotel building, creating one of the most stunning examples of neo-Gothic architecture ever seen. The workmanship inside and out is of the very highest standard and exemplary of Victorian style, craftsmanship and engineering.

# Cycle Hire
# Docking Station

## CAMDEN

Launched in the summer of 2010, the Barclays Cycle Hire scheme comprises 6,000 machines and 400 docking stations to provide a pay-and-go facility for everyone to use. They are affectionately known as 'Boris bikes' after the Mayor of London Boris Johnson (b. 1964), who introduced the scheme as part of a drive to ease traffic congestion and pollution in the city. The cycles, which are regularly checked and maintained, can be removed from one docking station and returned to another, with the first 30 minutes of use being free of charge.

# Waterloo Station

## LAMBETH

Looking at this magnificent terminal building, it is hard to imagine that in the late nineteenth century it was referred to as the 'most perplexing railway station in London'. This was due to various rail companies using the same facility, which led to a somewhat haphazard system of platforms. The station was redesigned in 1900 and 22 years later Queen Mary (1867–1953), consort to George V (1865–1936), opened the new Waterloo Station with the neatly aligned platforms that we see today. It is by far the busiest station in London and the second busiest in Europe.

# Thames River Cruises

## RIVER THAMES

One of the most enjoyable tourist experiences is to see London from the Thames, particularly as many of the most iconic buildings can be seen from here with uninterrupted views. Passing the Houses of Parliament, for example, one can see not only the true magnificence of these nineteenth-century buildings but in the summer months it is also possible to see Members of Parliament on the terraces overlooking the river enjoying a cup of tea. At the Tower of London too, one can see the king's private water-gate entrance, which has changed little since the thirteenth century.

# River Bus at Bankside Pier

## SOUTHWARK

The River Thames has been an underused resource for commuter traffic, but now it is enjoying something of a renaissance. River buses are operated by TfL, although there are other routes used by commuters and tourists. They are an alternative to the often crowded road buses and trains, and many are now equipped with catering facilities and wi-fi connections. There are over 20 boarding piers from Putney in the west right up to Greenwich and Docklands in the east, making it a viable option for many commuters.

# Bank Underground Station

CITY OF LONDON

One of the most heavily used stations, Bank emerges at the heart of the City of London, close to the Bank of England from where it gets its name. The station was formerly called 'City' when it provided an underground train link between Waterloo and this area, but changed its name in 1900 to accommodate the Northern and Central Line extensions. In a bombing raid in January 1941 the station took a direct hit that killed 57 people and created a crater above the ticket hall 100 metres across.

# Liverpool Street Station

CITY OF LONDON

One of the most poignant sculptures in London was unveiled outside Liverpool Street Station in 2006 to commemorate the 10,000 Jewish children evacuated from Nazi persecution in Germany and Eastern Europe, just before the outbreak of the Second World War. The rescue mission was known as the Kindertransport, during which many children arrived at this station prior to being 'adopted' by British families. Frank Meisler (b. 1929), who was one of the 'kindern' that found safety in Britain, created the sculpture, replacing an earlier version now in the Imperial War Museum.

# Canary Wharf Underground Station

## TOWER HAMLETS

The picture shows one of two huge canopy openings to Canary Wharf Station, built as part of the Jubilee Line extension to facilitate the many commuters who arrive here daily. These canopies, designed by Lord Foster, are sited on an east-west axis, their clever shape refracting natural light into the cavernous space beneath and separated by Jubilee Park above. The station was built after draining the 78-foot-deep water-filled dock that was in this location, and then providing an old-fashioned 'cut and cover' tunnel solution to its creation.

# Escalators at Canary Wharf

## TOWER HAMLETS

When the Underground station opened in 1999, it was estimated that 50,000 people would use this cavernous space every weekday. That figure was soon exceeded, and it is now thought that over 40 million people use the station every year, making it the busiest outside central London. With continued development in this area expected, the arrival of the new railway Crossrail cannot come quickly enough to relieve some of the pressure on the Jubilee Line. The station links to its Docklands Light Railway counterpart using the underground shopping malls.

# Cultural London

As a hotbed of cultural activity, London is probably unsurpassed. From the late sixteenth century, the city had its own markets for displaying and selling wares from exotic places. Many cultural artefacts are now displayed in the vast array of museums in London, from the intimate settings of Sir John Soane's House in Lincoln's Inn to the huge British Museum.

From the time of William Shakespeare, theatre has been a vibrant part of London's culture, with the West End providing a variety of shows from serious drama to musicals, Beckett to burlesque. Music, too, features in London, as it has done for at least 200 years. Many accomplished composers such as George Frideric Handel (1685–1759) came to the city to perform, and more recently musicians from America such as Lady Gaga have performed in London's O2 Arena.

Various cultures pervade the London scene, increasing its diversity, with major non-indigenous festivals now established in the city. The most vibrant of these is the annual Notting Hill Carnival, centred round the Afro-Caribbean community and a key component of London's culture since 1964.

# Portobello Road

## KENSINGTON AND CHELSEA

Portobello Road is home every Saturday to what is now recognized as the world's largest antique market, its outdoor stalls stretching for over half a mile. The market itself is about 150 years old, but in the mid-twentieth century antique dealers started arriving, a feature that has continued to grow. The street has featured in many films, most notably *Notting Hill*, made in 1999. The Electric Cinema, one of the country's oldest movie theatres, opened in Portobello Road in 1910 and is still in use today.

# Natural History Museum

## KENSINGTON AND CHELSEA

Having made the decision that the collection at the British Museum was getting too large, a new museum was envisaged to look after its growing collection of natural history exhibits. This stunning piece of late Victorian architecture is by Alfred Waterhouse (1830–1905). Not a devotee of one particular aesthetic, he fused Renaissance symmetry with a Romanesque style of rounded arches. The museum is home to over 70 million exhibits, including Dippy the diplodocus dinosaur skeleton in the central hall, and Archie the giant squid in the Darwin Centre.

# Victoria and Albert Museum

## KENSINGTON AND CHELSEA

The V&A is the world's largest museum of design and decorative arts. It was opened as the South Kensington Museum by Queen Victoria in 1857, largely funded by the profits from the 1851 Great Exhibition. The museum changed to its current name in 1899, when a new extension was being built to accommodate the growing collection. Among its most prized possessions are the Ardabil Carpet, the Great Bed of Ware and 20 sculptures by Rodin that the artist gifted to the museum.

# Royal Albert Hall

## CITY OF WESTMINSTER

The idea of a hall was first mooted by Prince Albert in 1851 but, owing to a lack of funds, the scheme was abandoned. After Albert's death in 1861, a public appeal was made for finance in which patrons would pay in advance for a life season ticket to events and concerts. The hall is affectionately known as the 'nation's village hall' because of its intimate atmosphere, despite it being large enough to accommodate over 5,000 people. Apart from concerts, the venue has been used for boxing, graduation ceremonies and the annual Festival of Remembrance.

# Tate Britain

## CITY OF WESTMINSTER

The building of a new gallery of British art was the result of the generosity of the millionaire sugar magnate Sir Henry Tate (1819–99), who donated his collection of 65 paintings provided they were housed in a fit-for-purpose gallery, to which he donated £80,000. The gallery is home to a remarkable collection of British art from the sixteenth century to the present day, with works by William Hogarth (1697–1764) and John Constable as well as contemporary artists such as Damien Hirst (b. 1965). Arguably its most important collection is the Turner Bequest.

# National Gallery
## CITY OF WESTMINSTER

Located along the northern edge of Trafalgar Square is the National Gallery, home to European art from the early Renaissance to 1900, including work by Leonardo da Vinci (1452–1519), Canaletto (1697–17) and Rubens (1577–1640), as well as the Impressionists, such as Camille Pissarro (1830–1903). The collection is one of the smallest of any national collection, comprising less than 2,500 paintings, and was one of the last to be founded, coming into existence only in 1824. During the Second World War the paintings were removed from the gallery and placed inside a slate quarry in Wales for safekeeping.

# Somerset House
## CITY OF WESTMINSTER

Despite being a major city in the eighteenth century, London did not have a substantial civic building until 1775, when the architect Sir William Chambers (1723–96) was commissioned to create the capital's first major public building. It has been home to many bodies such as the Royal Academy (1771–1836) and the Royal Society (1780–1857), as well as government offices such as the Registrar of Births, Deaths and Marriages (1836–1973). Today it is home to various public bodies as well as the Courtauld Institute of Art.

# Covent Garden Market
## CITY OF WESTMINSTER

Following the move of the fruit, vegetable and flower wholesale distribution market to Nine Elms, existing buildings at Covent Garden were refurbished in the 1970s and opened as a shopping centre in 1980. Since then it has been further enhanced and is the location for trendy shops, restaurants, bars and no shortage of street theatre to entertain visitors. One of the Victorian iron and glass buildings formerly used as a flower market is now home to the London Transport Museum, which was opened in 1980, but has been the subject of a recent major refurbishment.

# Tuttons in Covent Garden

## CITY OF WESTMINSTER

Tuttons has occupied this site in Covent Garden since the 1970s, when the market was still in operation, and continued after its refurbishment in 1980. It has an enviable reputation for good food. In the summer months the large doors slide back and there is a genuine feeling of dining *al fresco* even inside. Unlike many other restaurants, Tuttons is also open early in the morning for breakfast. There are also private dining areas such as the Vault for more intimate occasions.

# Floral Hall at the Royal Opera House

## CITY OF WESTMINSTER

The iron and glass structure known as the Floral Hall was created by the architect E.M. Barry (1830–80), the son of Sir Charles Barry who designed the Houses of Parliament. Built in 1858, it was originally part of the flower market in Covent Garden, adjacent to the rebuilt Royal Opera House. The building fell into disrepair after the market closed, but the refurbishment of the theatre in the 1990s included the Floral Hall thanks to a donation from the Paul Hamlyn Foundation.

# Leicester Square

## CITY OF WESTMINSTER

The Odeon Cinema Leicester Square, being the largest single-screen theatre in Britain, is the setting for many film premieres, including the entire Harry Potter series, as well as the annual Royal Film Performance. The square has been the home for entertainment since the nineteenth century, with large theatres such as the Alhambra and the Empire Theatre, which later became a cinema capable of showing 70-mm epics such as *Lawrence of Arabia* and musicals such as *The Sound of Music*. In the middle of the square is a statue of Charlie Chaplin (1889–1977).

# Shaftesbury Avenue

## CITY OF WESTMINSTER

At the centre of London's Theatreland or West End is Shaftesbury Avenue, laid out between 1877 and 1886 as a project to clear slums in the area and to provide an arterial road for increased volumes of traffic. Along the avenue itself there are four theatres in close proximity opened between 1888 and 1907, and another further along at the junction with Charing Cross Road. The Palace, opened in 1891 as an opera house, is now owned and run as one of The Really Useful Group Theatres, owned by Lord Andrew Lloyd Webber (b. 1948).

APOLLO
APOLLO THEATRE
DAVID SUCHET
ZOË WANAMAKER
ARTHUR MILLER'S
ALL MY SONS
HOWARD DAVIES
HAIR
HAIR
HAIR
HAIR
GIELGUD
THEATRE
HAIR
HAIR
HAIR
DANGEROUS ★ DIRTY DIANA plus many more!
V544 DGT
56120

# Piccadilly Art Market

## CITY OF WESTMINSTER

A familiar sight on Saturdays and Sundays along Piccadilly are paintings and photographs hung on the railings of Green Park. There are also books for sale, as well as antique prints. The traders pay for their pitch and turn up in vans to unload their pictures before hanging them on the railings. There are also similar pitches along the Bayswater Road on the northern edge of Hyde Park, and the concept has been copied in several other towns and cities in Britain during the summer months.

# Regent Street

## CITY OF WESTMINSTER

The Christmas lights in Regent Street being switched on by a celebrity is an eagerly anticipated event each year, a tradition dating back to 1948. The street was substantially rebuilt between 1895 and 1927 to include several large department stores such as Dickens and Jones, Swan and Edgar, and Hamleys. Only Hamleys – the largest toyshop in the world – remains. Although it is actually in Great Marlborough Street, Liberty's department store, opened in 1875, is always associated with the Regent Street shops.

# Oxford Street

## CITY OF WESTMINSTER

At nearly one and a half miles long, Oxford Street is one of the longest shopping streets, and certainly the busiest, in Europe. Due to the volume of pedestrians, access for vehicles to most of the street is restricted except for buses and taxis. There are several large stores in Oxford Street including Debenhams, John Lewis and the flagship store for Marks and Spencer. The largest of the stores is Selfridges, which opened its doors in 1909, and was among the first to recognize the sales potential of appealing to the 'new woman'.

# British Museum

## CAMDEN

A museum of the world, for the world, it has a collection in excess of six million artefacts attracting over six million visitors from the four corners of the earth. The British Museum was created in 1753 from the collection of London physician Sir Hans Sloane, which has been added to by other renowned collectors such as Sir William Hamilton (1730–1803), who donated his series of ancient Greek vases, and King George III, who bequeathed his library. Among the museum's most treasured possessions are the Rosetta Stone and the Parthenon Marbles.

# Great Court at the British Museum

## CAMDEN

When the British Library was created in 1997 and the books transferred from the Reading Room at the British Museum, a decision was made to re-use the space by redeveloping the site. The Great Court was opened in 2000 by HM The Queen to much acclaim for the designer Lord Foster who, using the old Reading Room as a central hub, created a light and airy circular public space with easier accessibility into the public galleries and a staircase to the upstairs galleries.

# Charles Dickens Museum

## CAMDEN

The writer Charles Dickens lived in this house for nearly three years between 1837 and 1839, during which time he wrote two of his novels, *Oliver Twist* and *Nicholas Nickleby*, and completed *The Pickwick Papers*. The Dickenses had only been married for a year when they moved in and already had the first of 10 children, with two more born while the family were living at this house. Also living in the house was his sister-in-law Anne, who died in Dickens' arms, an incident that inspired his character Little Nell in the novel *The Old Curiosity Shop*.

# Royal Festival Hall

## LAMBETH

In 1951 London staged the Festival of Britain to celebrate the centenary of the Great Exhibition and to promote good design in the rebuilding programme following the Second World War. The event was staged along the south bank of the Thames and ran during the summer months of that year. Most of the buildings were temporary structures except the Royal Festival Hall, which is still in use today as a concert venue and provided the impetus for other arts-related buildings in the area now known as the South Bank.

# National Theatre

## LAMBETH

One of the venues to be created in the South Bank arts complex was the National Theatre, now known as the Royal National Theatre. It was completed in 1977 to a design by the English architect Sir Denys Lasdun (1914–2001) in a Brutalist style that Prince Charles (b. 1948) compared to a nuclear power station. The first artistic director of the 'National' was Lord Olivier, who is commemorated with a statue outside and in the name of the main auditorium. There are two other auditoriums making up the complex.

# Old Vic

## LAMBETH

Prior to its own home being built, the National Theatre used the Old Vic, an early nineteenth-century theatre that was renowned for its company of players that included Sir John Gielgud (1904–2000), and their performances of Shakespeare's plays under the management of Lilian Baylis (1874–1937). She was also responsible for revitalizing the Sadler's Wells Theatre and creating what became the English National Opera. The current director of the Old Vic is the American actor Kevin Spacey (b. 1959), who has also starred in productions, most notably his Shakespearean debut as Richard II in 2005.

# Lord Mayor's Show Celebrations

## CITY OF LONDON

Each year during November the City of London celebrates the appointment of the new Lord Mayor of London, who is elected the previous September. The day begins with a pageant through the City with the Mayor in his gold coach joining the procession as it passes his official residence, Mansion House. The procession, which consists of a series of floats, with liverymen from the different ancient Guilds, makes its way to the Royal Courts of Justice, where the Mayor takes his oath of allegiance to the Crown.

# Barbican Centre

## CITY OF LONDON

The area of Cripplegate in the City of London was virtually destroyed during the Blitz and was left as urban wasteland until the 1960s, when the Barbican development began. It comprises the Barbican residential estate, consisting of three tower blocks of apartments and some low-rise housing, totalling just over 2,000 homes; and the Barbican Arts Centre containing a conference venue, trade halls, a concert hall that is home to the London Symphony Orchestra, three cinemas, two theatres and an art gallery, making it the largest performing arts complex in Europe.

# Museum of London
## CITY OF LONDON

As part of the Barbican development, the Museum of London was opened in 1976 to provide a history of the city in chronological order, a presentation strategy that continues today. The location of the museum has facilitated a viewing gallery across an area where part of a Roman barbican (an outer fortification) can be seen. The museum contains many artefacts that have been collected and preserved by the Museum of London Archaeology Service (MOLAS), the body responsible for uncovering London's past history at construction sites in the city.

# Pearly Kings and Queens Harvest Festival
## CITY OF LONDON

The first Pearly King of London was Henry Croft (1862–1930), a roadsweeper who collected money for charity in the late nineteenth century. His friends were market traders, or costermongers, who by tradition sewed pearl buttons on their sleeves as a status symbol. Occasionally some would fall off and Croft would collect these while sweeping and sew them onto his own jacket, eventually covering it. He wore the jacket when collecting for charity, establishing a tradition in London for pearly kings and queens in different areas to raise money for good causes.

# Tate Modern

## SOUTHWARK

This former oil-fired power station was transformed into one of the most-visited museums in London and the most-visited gallery of modern art in the world. It has been so successful that a new wing is currently under construction, increasing its exhibition space by 50,000 square feet to accommodate other art forms such as performance. Existing displays are of international modern art of the twentieth century, including many contemporary works by living artists. It is also planned to incorporate recreational areas around the gallery as part of the ongoing revitalization of Southwark.

# Hay's Galleria

## SOUTHWARK

In a former life this covered area was an enclosed dock and storage area for dry goods such as the tea that was brought into the Pool of London. This dock was affectionately known as the 'Larder of London'. It had to be rebuilt in 1861 because of a disastrous fire in Tooley Street that claimed many other buildings, and was used regularly until it was again virtually destroyed in the Blitz. Today it is a thriving shopping mall and restaurant area, part of the regeneration programme that has revitalized this area.

# St Katherine Docks

## TOWER HAMLETS

These docks were built in 1828 and used for the import of expensive commodities such as ivory and marble right up to the 1930s when it went into decline, finally closing in 1968. The area was substantially redeveloped and now incorporates luxury apartments, once the Ivory House warehouse, that overlook a marina for yachts. Around the quay are a number of shops and restaurants, making this an ideal leisure location that is often used to stage corporate events because of its close proximity to the City.

# Dickens Inn at St Katherine Docks

## TOWER HAMLETS

Surrounded by the new developments at St Katherine Docks is the Dickens Inn public house and restaurant. Originally in a different location within the docks, the building has been reconstructed on this site using the original materials. The refurbished pub was opened in 1976 by the grandson of Charles Dickens, who thought his grandfather would have approved of the galleried façade. The pub is very popular with the locals and is visited by many tourists, who have learned of its reputation for good beer.

# Petticoat Lane Market

## TOWER HAMLETS

One of several markets established east of the City, Petticoat Lane can trace its history back to Tudor times, although it was not regulated until the 1930s. This area has always been associated with the clothing industry, hence its name, with immigrants arriving here because of the commercial possibilities and relatively cheap rents. The market was popular when Sunday trading was illegal, as Jewish merchants who did not observe the same Sabbath day would open for business. Today, other ethnic minorities run many of the stalls.

# O2 Arena

## GREENWICH

The Millennium Dome was created for the year 2000 celebrations, but thereafter came to be regarded as something of a white elephant. However, following a spectacular transformation and an opening concert by Bon Jovi in 2007, it has become one of the most popular music venues in the world. The complex will also be used for some events in the 2012 London Olympics, but will temporarily be known as the North Greenwich Arena because of a conflict in sponsorship deals. In addition to the concert space there is also an 11-screen cinema within the complex.

# Index